D0104793

The Law
Of
Achievement

The Law Of Achievement

Discover Your
Purpose, Possibility and Potential

Kathleen Gage   Lori Giovannoni

Maxwell Publishing
12610 South 700 East
Draper, Utah 84020

Cover illustration and layout by Karen Noel © 2006
All Rights Reserved.

Editing by Lisa Workman, Workman Central.

ISBN 978-0-9658159-6-3

1. Inspirational   2. Business   3. Spiritual

"You will not discover your greatness by emulating someone else.
You will only know your greatness by being who you are."

~ Kathleen Gage ~

How the book came to be...

The idea for this book began many years ago as a result of numerous conversations. Having both achieved multiple levels of success, we wanted to share with others what achievement meant to us. Although we knew someday we would write the book we were continually sidetracked with never-ending professional endeavors.

We went from thinking about writing the book to being guided to write the book through one event that changed the course of many lives. It is through this event our belief that the only point of power is in the now was reinforced like never before.

At 6:19 pm on September 2, 2005, our world stopped. Troy Roper Jr., Lori's husband and Kathleen's dear friend, was in a severe motorcycle accident. The pursuit of business, joint ventures and material concerns came to a screaming halt.

For 102 days our lives revolved around the shock trauma unit, surgery, intensive care, doctors, nurses and an endless stream of visitors and well wishers. Lori slept in Troy's room every night and Kathleen relieved Lori every day.

There was no word or concern about business issues. Priorities were rearranged and the world had shifted on its axis. When the crisis subsided it was evident we all had changed. Our beliefs and values had been tempered and some of them changed completely. Our greatest lesson and realization is that far too often we had lived in "someday." Troy's accident reminded us to live in today, cherishing each moment. After over eight months of recovery, Troy continues to inspire us.

People tend to put off until "someday" what they really would like to do today. The delays come for many reasons. Time, money, laziness, no sense of urgency or just plain not getting around to it.

Starting as a someday project that we dabbled with for years, Troy's accident transformed this book into a today project. When we sat down to write *The Law of Achievement*, we knew it was destined to be a book that impacted many and made a difference not only to its readers but to people outside of the traditional business market.

Looking to transform lives with the book's message as well as the proceeds, we chose to partner with Executive Women International® (EWI) and contribute a portion of each book sale to the Reading Rally.

Both of us understand the power of the written and spoken word. We have made our living from both for decades. To think of a life without the ability to read is almost beyond our comprehension and yet, we know this is a fact of life for many.

Having both been members of this fine organization for many years, facilitating EWI's Annual Leadership Conference and having a lot of respect for the Reading Rally program, it made perfect sense to partner with EWI.

It is through the support of countless individuals and the experience of the now moment that this book came to be. Our intention in writing *The Law of Achievement* is to fuel action, inspire dreams and assist others in living a life of purpose, possibility and potential.

This book is dedicated to...

Troy Lee Roper, Jr., who has more courage and will than any man I know. Thank you for coming back to us, for holding on so tight and for loving us so well. You will have the wind at your back one day soon, my love.

Lori Giovannoni-Roper

This book is also dedicated to people everywhere who live a life of achievement often with little or no recognition. To the unsung heroes who daily bless the lives of others through their courage, willingness to walk through incredibly difficult situations, and somehow manage to live a life with incredible dignity.

It is in their willingness to fulfill their destiny they are a shining example of how one can live their purpose, possibility and potential.

Kathleen Gage

With gratitude...

I'd like to acknowledge the many people in our lives who made the days bearable and the journey back to life memorable. Chris and Maggie Roper, for being there every step of the way; you were a continual reminder of grace and love. Thanks to the folks that started the unimaginable journey with us that began on September 2, 2006 and never left our side:

Frank and Sue Arnold
Judy Wolf
Matt Wilson
Ron and Meg Schmidt
Polly and Rod Johnson
Sam and Becky Guevara
Carol and Jim Hoard
Lynda and Dave Jeppesen
Karen Noel & Kathleen Gage
Marjeane Daniels
Marv and Harriett Brittenham
Michael Giovannoni
Sandy Hatcher, Houston EWI
Deb Taylor, Dallas EWI
The EWI Corporate Staff
EWI Representatives throughout the nation who held us in their prayers.
The Beehive Beamers
Maxine and Marv Turner, who made Christmas magical.

Lori Giovannoni

A heartfelt thanks...

To all who have influenced me throughout my life who taught me what true achievement means. A special thanks to the thousands of people who have been in my audiences and allowed me to share my thoughts and words through the privilege of the platform.

My deepest thanks, appreciation, and love to Karen Noel, for the talents you constantly amaze me with. This book would not have happened without your vision, support and belief. I am grateful for all you bring to my life.

To my mother and father, Jeanne and David Gage, for being my heroes and instilling values that I respect and appreciate; my sister, Patricia Twitchell, for your love, friendship and willingness to listen and your love of bears; my sister, Lorraine Lawson, for all you contribute to my life and the beauty you bring to the world in your art; to Kathleen Elsten for showing me what achievement means no matter how great the odds; Patrick McGoey who is an amazing example of what it means to manifest our desires; Nettie Apland for teaching me that any mountain can be climbed one step at a time; Troy Roper for showing me what true courage means, Lori Giovannoni for your commitment to your word, Celeste and Sandra for all your support, and for my special friends who make my life complete. You know who you are.

A Special thanks to the EWI Executive Team, Chapter Presidents and the EWI Board of Directors.

To Kathryn, Bon Mama, Granny, Van Andreasen and Robert Leach who continue to inspire me to untold places from your space in the heavens.

Kathleen Gage

Purposely Kind

Kindness is an achievement few of us master

It is rare that we meet a wholly kind person. We have pockets of kindness reserved for special people and situations, but to be wholly kind is difficult. It requires commitment and purposeful actions. So many of our unkind actions stem from the unconscious: a spoken word that wounds in a split second; an off-handed remark makes haste toward the intended target; the temptation of innuendo that cannot be resisted only to land at the feet of one who understands all to well.

Kindness requires vigilance and intention, the kind of intention that means you've done something on purpose. It requires the ability to act, opposed to reacting from a small and demanding ego. Kindness is an intelligent man's behavior, one that springs from the understanding that we live in a connected universe where there is no "us and them."

The measurement of a kind person is in not found in one special relationship or in a particularly compelling situation. Kindness can only be measured in the daily habits of living. Living a purposely kind life is an acquired taste.

Imagine if our only life's purpose was kindness. How much easier life could be and how much more we could accomplish if we lived in a place of purposeful kindness.

How kind do you find yourself to be daily, hourly, or moment to moment?

The Power of Potential

Each of us is said to possess potential

Much of our life's journey is dedicated to making use of this unexpressed possibility. Should we choose to ignore the demands of our potential, we are referred to as an underachiever, breaking the unspoken law of achievement.

Mothers want their children to possess and achieve their deepest potential. Teachers speak of students as "possessing so much potential." Family members shake their head in disappointment when a member of the family does not rise to their expectation, lamenting that, "It is such a waste of potential." What is this nebulous quality that is naturally mourned when lost?

Potential is the instinctive understanding that life is a gift and each person living his or her life is experiencing a one-time, unrepeatable event, never to take place in the history of the universe again.

Potential is the spiritual understanding that your view of the world is unique and that you are precious. Your view is not to be found anywhere but in your presence. It is simply the hope that each of us moves the other forward in self-love and consciousness through the expression of all we can be.

"The greatest achievement of all is the ability to help others realize their fullest potential."
Linda M. Lentini President 2005 - 2006
EWI Washington, DC Chapter

Living a Possibility

So many possibilities, so little time

Our lives are notoriously busy, bowing to the requirement of a high-speed a life. We refer to our work as "busy-ness" often confusing action for achievement and many commitments as living a life of possibilities.

The more we do the busy-er we are, with less time to get things done. "Having it All" became the battle cry of the successful. Living a life of possibility was measured by the things we owned. The problem being, of course, that all possessions eventually lose their attraction. Years of busy-ness can leave us materially successful but soul weary.

True possibility is as elusive as potential and as faint as a morning dream. The minute you live the possibility it leaves the realm of "what if" and becomes the reality of the moment. It isn't in chasing possibilities that we find our greatest satisfaction, but rather in taking the time to create an environment of limitless possibilities so life is a journey of choice not a race we will never win.

Possibilities, like people, require nurturing and a place to grow. Our minds house all possibilities, but access to them calls for a particular kind of self-love and personal knowledge. Knowing how and when to call forth the possibilities of your day or your life is an art. There are no project plans, goal setting courses or prioritized lists that will teach us to reach into our self and elicit the possibilities of our being.

This is personal work; the personal work of self-care, both simultaneously powerful and fragile. Possibility must be cultivated until there is a strength that allows it to stand on its own.

The Illusion of Certainty

Achievement is revealed in uncertainty

Nothing in this world is certain, but we expend a tremendous amount of effort in an attempt to create certainty. In some respects you might say that success and achievement minimize the potential for risk in life and ensure the experience of certainty.

To ensure certainty some of us take jobs that promise a paycheck every two weeks. We send our children to schools with a history of certainty to ensure their academic success. Creating certainty is done with the best of intentions and a desire to minimize life struggles for those we love. We try to diminish the sense of the unknown. We sometimes become habitual in establishing and creating routines to avoid the unknown. There are many ways to add certainty to an uncertain life, at least for the moment. Yet we are reminded on a daily basis that absolute certainty is fleeting at best.

It is the very uncertainty of life that has us love with intensity, live with passion and cherish the moments that may have passed unnoticed if each moment were guaranteed to be followed by the next. It is the uncertainty of life that pushes us to achieve.

A Purposeful Silence

Possibility lives within silence

Throughout history there is ample evidence that a groundswell of possibility lives within silence. When life is overwhelming, a moment or two of silence may work wonders. But, like relaxation, there seems to be little time for such an indulgence.

Silence seems such a luxury when so many other things demand our attention. To stop all movement, calm our thoughts and wait for the dawning of the mind seems like a luxury afforded only to those that have dedicated their lives to a religion or form of silent meditation. Nevertheless, most of us recognize that silence is like water for the spirit and without it we cannot fully bloom.

The lack of silence produces a deficiency like the

lack of an essential nutrient. A lack of silence will create a low tolerance for stillness and render us deaf to our own callings and needs. We must discipline ourselves to drink from this well and to refresh our spirit.

At first the silence only brings more noise; we hear the clutter of our mind, the list of endless things we could be doing instead. But eventually things settle down and in the silence we find ourselves again.

Bathed in silence our true self begins to speak for it knows there is a presence to hear.

Anticipation and Achievement

*Anticipation opens the possibility
of achievement*

L ike a child anticipates Christmas, a life filled with achievement is also filled with anticipation. The innocence of a child allows for the belief of something good to come: a Christmas morning filled with the joy of gifts, validation of their existence and recognition of their place in the family.

After a time Christmas becomes commercialized and Santa eventually fades away into the memories of our childhood. It is not the innocent belief in Santa we miss, it is the innocent belief we can receive gifts merely because we exist.

Anticipation and achievement come from a belief in the goodness and abundance of the universe. Like children, we need touchstones and rituals to keep our natural state of anticipation alive. We need stories to remind us of our capability and the rewards for our existence.

Begin the day in an anticipatory state of joy and blessings, expecting the best throughout the day.

"Believe in yourself, do your best at all times, making sure nothing you do will hurt someone else in the process."
Sybil Adkins 2005 - 2006 President
EWI Orlando Chapter

Faith -The Foundation of Achievement

Faith is not solely reserved for the realm of the spiritual

Faith allows us to cross all boundaries of limitation. Faith in ourselves is as important as a faith in something larger than self. It is a prerequisite of life calling upon the possibilities that have yet to be brought into existence.

We talk about "believing in ourselves," "trusting ourselves," and sometimes "having faith in ourselves," but where do we look for an example of this faith? How are we taught to have an understanding of self so strong it is not shaken by failure or rejection, not shattered by fear or lost to desire? Who teaches us to have faith in ourselves regardless of the outcome or situation?

Our life will be filled with many teachers. Our wisest teachers are those we love and those that love us.

Relationships grounded in love bring an unbending faith in each other. Having someone who can see your potential when you cannot and hold the faith that you will achieve the heights intended is the purpose of our relationships. We see these relationships in great teachers with their students, parents with their children, spouses with one another.

We all have evidence of how reliable and faithful we are when the chips are down. In looking for a little self-faith, the evidence is as close as an experience when we doubted we had the strength to get through but did so anyway.

Faith in another is a great gift; faith in self is even greater. Our lives are filled with memories of faith. We need only remember.

The Purpose of Frustration

Frustration, a catalyst for achievement

Some hold the belief that achievement always brings satisfaction. In reality, the opposite may be true.

Have you noticed how dissatisfied many people are with their lives? People who have achieved levels of material success and accomplishment, and yet, for some reason, there is an emptiness inside and a sense of incompleteness. Life seems somewhat out of balance.

This unbalance may well be the catalyst for expansion into more of your divine self. Evidence may appear when you notice relationships feeling out of step, as if you are traveling down one path while others are traveling another. You may intuitively know there is knowledge awaiting you, but you are not sure where to gain it. Some accomplishments may have lost their purpose and brought you back to where you started.

These occurrences are common to countless people. Many fear they are alone in this journey. As someone initially begins their journey down a more sacred and spiritual path, a course that leads to one's purpose, it may appear as if they are alone; as if what was familiar and made sense up to this point no longer seems to fit. All of your achievements may seem senseless and you struggle to find a new purpose.

The more you learn to trust the process of self-discovery, the more you will attract people and situations that will accelerate your growth. As you travel the various roads of your spiritual path you will realize this is not a solitary journey.

It is this realization that allows frustration to be a catalyst for achievement.

Meditation and Achievement

Moments of silence reveal our purpose

A common belief of many is that meditation is reserved solely as a spiritual practice. Although meditation is a spiritual ritual, it can also be a strong catalyst for achievement.

Many forms of meditation involve the following elements:

+ Rhythmic Breathing
+ Listening in the silence
+ "Going within" or reflecting upon the silence

If you are at a point in your life where things seem slightly askew and you don't know what to do, sometimes the best action to take is no action. Sit quietly and let the answers come from within.

How do we accomplish meditative practices that have become misplaced in an action driven and result measured world?

Like everything that becomes part of who we are, we must start with small steps. Even a minute of deep breathing before you start your day will eventually bring results, but only with practice.

Exchange a minute of worry and frenzy for a moment of silence and watch your world slowly change.

The Purpose of Destiny

Destiny is a process of flow
rather than an act of force

Achievement comes from the knowledge that we
have the ability to shape our destiny based on our
beliefs, attitudes and actions. Many of us have been
trained to utilize the power of our beliefs through force,
with undeniable results.

Force alone lends itself to fatigue and burnout.
Actions based solely on force are founded in a belief
that there is not enough, that we live in a world which is
hostile and aggressive. There is a powerful source that
compliments actions of force. It is the understanding
that achievement can be grounded in the spiritual.

A belief in force alone demands personal
recognition to maintain a sense of self. When actions
are led by our gentler side, the side of us that remains

connected to the heavens, results require less effort and are more satisfying.

"Achievement can be described in one word - character. Every day we are challenged either in our professional or personal life. How a person handles the challenges shows the true evidence of their character. Achievement in life requires a passion for happiness, change, success, learning opportunities and life itself. Your ability will take you to the top. Your character will keep you there"

Hazel Thomas 2005 - 2006 President

EWI Little Rock Chapter

The Power of the Moment

*Moment by moment we create
our lives*

There is magic in the moment. When we live in the moment, we are alert to all possibility. We become the recipient of potential and a spectator of purpose. Being in the moment means we are in the experience rather than thinking about it. This kind of presence opens an awareness filled with possibility and the hope of achievement.

This moment links us between heaven and earth and allows a life that is continually dynamic and fluid. As thrilling as it is to live in the now, it often escapes us, shoved aside by regrets of the past and visions of the future.

Continually living in memories of the past and thoughts of the future is hard on the body, mind and soul. When we are absent to the moment we are more susceptible to danger; we are distracted and not attentive.

When we are absent to the moment, we become exhausted on an emotional and physical level. Not the kind of exhaustion that comes from a good day's work or play. It is the kind of exhaustion that no matter how much rest or sleep you get, you are still tired.

A life filled with energy and light is a life lived in the moment. Even the toughest of times take on a sacred quality that calls upon strength granted to the conscious.

Achieving Joy

Joy is a perpetual meditation

There is a definite joy in the satisfaction of achievement and there is a definite satisfaction in the achievement of joy.

Thinking that joy is externally motivated, many achievers are on a continual quest to find the next accomplishment, experience or relationship that will bring lasting joy. Searching for joy in all the wrong places eventually brings us to questions, "Where does joy reside? How do I make joy a continual part of my life? How do I achieve an emotional state of joy and have a *lightness of being* regardless of my circumstances?"

The joy of life lies in the choices we make. How we react, regardless of the situation, creates the next emotion, the next moment and all the moments that follow. We create our happiness or sadness, anger or love, apathy or joy.

Joy requires self control, a willingness to have life at its best and an understanding that the universe responds to joy with limitless possibilities.

Joy is a perpetual meditation!

"Happiness is the sign of success."
Doris Bobadilla 2005 - 2006 President
EWI New Orleans Chapter

The Influence of Beliefs

We are all champions in the making

It is clear there is no definitive answer as to how much or little we influence our lives with our beliefs, only that there is a degree of influence. As the scientist's beliefs and expectation impacts their experiment in the world of quantum physics, our expectations certainly influence our experiment called "life."

The question simply becomes, "To what degree do I choose to believe?"

Does believing in our thoughts, meditations, and prayers increase the quality of life and the frequency of our achievements? Ask any world champion. A champion can tame their mind to be an advocate at all times regardless of the situation. A champion is one who understands that time is fleeting and life is rich with possibility. A champion is a champion first in their mind and heart long before they are a champion in the sport.

We are all champions in the making. All we have to do is *believe.*

---

*"What I know about achievement, I learned as a child from Edgar A. Guest's poem **It Couldn't Be Done**. The core of the message is, "If you tackle the thing that couldn't be done without any doubting or "quit-it"- then you'll do it!" No matter what you attempt to accomplish, you cannot achieve that which you do not believe."*

Betty J. Goodman 2005 - 2006 President
EWI Cleveland Chapter

The Potential for Abundance

When a heart feels abundant the world is a rich and generous place

A bundance. Such a lovely word. Filled with promise and joy we utter the word like a mantra, hoping with focus and attention our lives will become the true manifestation of that which we so clearly crave. We want an abundance of things and money and experience. A life filled with choices all offering us the joy of limitless possibilities and the means by which to live.

Millions have taken seminars to create abundance. Some have perfected their mental focus intensely to look for evidence of riches. And many others have simply accepted feeling as though abundance is not a part of their life and to devote time and attention to it is simply nonsense. Nonetheless we are bombarded with images of the abundant life.

Unfortunately abundance is usually translated into the current norm and labeled something it is not. Typically seen as having a lot of something, we rely on our eyes to tell us if we are experiencing abundance through achievements.

Much of an abundant life is in the realm of the invisible; absent from the balance sheet of accomplishments and acquisitions. Abundance is as much a feeling as a state of ownership.

When a heart feels abundant the world is a rich and generous place.

An Attitude of Innocence

So much achievement is driven by an attempt to redeem the human spirit

We work hard to prove our worth, to find love and experience approval. We spend our life establishing our place in the world and then use the rest of it to defend it.

A child does not sense their faults. Embarrassment and shame do not accompany the infant experience. What if we were like little children, trusting in our goodness and willing to receive what the world has to offer? Imagine what would be possible if we lived from a place of innocence and a sense that we are inherently good. Would that change the way you hold yourself and others?

What if you found that there is no grade given for your life because as a student of life you already have an A? Rosamund Stone Zander and Benjamin Zander, authors of the book *The Art of Possibility*, give their students an A and then request they perform into their A rather than chase a grade for an entire semester. The bell curve is straightened and the students are joyfully achieving heights of performance that inspired all.

We should give ourselves a break - an A at the beginning of our life. This doesn't mean we do not work hard or expend effort, it means that the effort expended is for the highest of achievements and that is the approval of self. The days of performing based upon fear, consequences and a sense of insufficiency will become obsolete.

Standing Still

We all experience periods of apparent stagnation

At a time of visible stillness change remains a constant, flowing in several directions and through many channels.

It is in our moments of stillness we seem to experience crucial and necessary growth. A lack of movement will eventually result in movement. Stillness gives way to change and change is the teacher of all.

Some believe their primary role to be that of the changer in the lives of others while others embrace the position of being changed. Each of us will experience both roles. There comes a time in life when even the changer must realize the need to be the changed.

There is no doubt that even the most powerful and influential teachers (changers) at some point must become the student (changed).

"Achievement is accomplished with the love, support and guidance of those around. With these, anything can be achieved."

Terry Muglia 2005 – 2006 President
EWI Chicago Chapter

The Purpose of Life

Life is but a moment in time

L ife is just a fleeting moment. This we know to be true. And yet in that moment so much occurs.

- Joy
- Love
- Excitement
- Pain
- Happiness
- Fear

We are on this earth for an undisclosed period of time. It is ours to make the most of and so often fear holds us back from doing all we are intended to do. If we could just realize that this body is only temporary housing.

Life is an opportunity for our spirit to evolve and our love to grow.

Inspired Moments

Inspiration surrounds us if we only take notice

Where does inspiration come from? Great scholars report a variety of sources from other people to dreams, from great works to humble moments. Some say a grateful heart is gifted with inspiration.

There seems to be a myriad of sources one can look to. The frustration lies in moving from searching for inspiration to becoming inspired. One is an issue of action and the other a process of reception.

Moments of inspiration and creative thought are gifts to the grateful. Be inspired.

Worry

*Freedom from worry is one of
life's great achievements*

As humans we are driven to worry. Aware of the precarious nature of life, worry comes naturally, but at a high cost. Worry drains our energy and depletes our spirit; even in the most dire of times searching for solutions or asking for understanding stands miles above the chronic and habitual thoughts of worry.

Many of us confuse worry with responsibility. We assume that if we worry we are dedicating a kind of attention that is demanded by the significance of the situation, but we are kidding ourselves. Responsibility has to do with conscious choice and has nothing to do with chronic worry. In fact there are times where the most responsible thing you can do is NOT worry.

Some people worry simply to beat the next problem

to the punch line. If they are worried before it occurs, one can feel justified. Funny how the problem matches the prediction.

When achievement is driven by worry it is difficult to enjoy. Each achievement leads to a new and different kind of concern that begs us to worry again.

A life full of achievement accompanied by a life full of worry is no life at all.

Gratitude

A grateful heart cannot be a hateful heart

We achieve our highest level of potential when we live in a state of gratitude.

As you move through the day, do your eyes see the best of things, grateful for the beauty of the day and the possibilities it holds? Or have your eyes become accustomed to seeing what is missing, searching for disappointment and evidence of lack?

At times it takes extreme effort to have the experience of gratitude. At other times it is not difficult at all. The paradox of gratitude is the more you express and live in gratitude the more you see what you have to be grateful for.

It is easy to be joyful and grateful when we have all we believe we deserve. It is in times of lack, pain, sorrow and loss that we are truly tested in our ability to be grateful.

Gratitude is an exercise of focus:

- Focus on your achievements rather than your failures.
- Focus on what is working rather than what is not.
- Focus on what you have, rather than what you don't.
- Focus on your heart rather than your head.

The Potential in Relationships

By ourselves we accomplish nothing

Our achievements are directly related to the relationships we have created and the quality of support they provide.

Relationships are not about being with people just like ourselves. Rather it is a respect for individualism and diversity. Just as a seed needs nurturing and care to grow, so do relationships. If we do not give a seed the care it needs, it will not grow and may possibly die. The same is also true for the relationships in our lives.

Think about the relationships in your life. Are you nurturing them to their highest level of possibility? The level of commitment we make to one another allows for the unfolding of any relationship.

The way we recognize our potential is by its

reflection in others. Other's mirror back to us our beliefs and self-worth. When we live in a vacuum void of relationships, we have no reflection.

"The continuous lifetime journey to make a difference to all of those who we serve by ever changing our vision and goals to reach new heights.....in the hopes that in the end one's life has made a positive impact on the lives of others and helped to shape a more positive world as well as developing positive relationships along the way. This is achievement."

Jo Ann Allen Nyquist 2005 - 2006 President
EWI Detroit-Windsor Chapter

Expansion

Potential is determined by your ability to expand beyond what is comfortable

Like the universe, we are either in a state of expansion or contraction at any given time.

In order to achieve our fullest potential we have to be willing to expand our actions beyond our present state of comfort. As the old saying goes, "If you always do what you did, you'll always get what you got."

It is in our willingness to do things that are unknown and unfamiliar that we experience a new side of ourselves.

Expansion is a state of acceptance and a willingness to step outside of what is comfortable in order to experience what is possible.

The Achievement of Responsibility

Freedom lies in your ability to respond

Taking responsibility for making things better requires a high level of willingness and integrity.

Continually stepping up to our responsibilities may feel daunting, but like sticking with any routine, what was difficult at first is liberating at last.

It is in your ability to respond from a place of truth high achievement is possible.

Miracles Happen

Even the smallest of achievements can be considered a miracle

Miracles happen, but we don't know when they will appear. Sometimes miracles happen as a result of expressing our hidden potential and believing in unseen possibilities. But we are impatient. Waiting is not our game and we want results immediately. Our inability to be patient may cause us to lose the miracle.

When the rewards are not quick enough or the pain is too great the temptation is to quit. Resist the urge to throw in the towel. Give yourself a little more time and effort. Don't quit five minutes before the miracle. You may find yourself pleasantly surprised.

"When you honor yourself by reaching deep within to accomplish something you didn't think was possible, that is an achievement. Just like miracles, achievements can be large or small. When life has been particularly hard, it might be an achievement to simply get up to face yet another day."

Mary Young 2005 - 2006 President
EWI Kansas City Chapter

The Purpose of Letting Go

*Letting go of outcomes allows
your purpose to unfold*

Our culture is driven by words like "surrender" and phrases like "letting go" which grate against the very nature of the high achiever. We have been bombarded with expressions like, "Quitters never win and winners never quit."

How easy would it all be if life were a matter of clichés? But clichés don't tell the whole story. In everyone's life there will be times and reasons for quitting, results in letting go and moments of quiet surrender.

The Purpose of Mentoring

Teachers come from the most unexpected places

Having or being a mentor is nothing new and certainly not unique to the high achiever. Mentors come in many forms and disguises, sometimes officially labeling the relationship as Mentor and Mentee. At others times both remain anonymous. But this is not a relationship to be taken lightly.

The mentor/mentee relationship can change the course of a life. A mentor can influence through their words, kindness and insight. As a mentor shares their experiences and wisdom with the mentee, the mentor is brought face-to-face with his/her beliefs and values, reinforcing them as they go and grow.

This is really a student-teacher relationship. It has been said, "When the student is ready the teacher appears." By the same token, "When the teacher is ready, the student appears."

"Achievements are vital to any organization, company or individual. When achievements are realized there is a sense of pride and accomplishment as well as motivation to keep the momentum going!"

Heather P. Harrison 2005 - 2006 President

EWI Seattle Chapter

The Birth of Possibility

*Create an environment of safety
and nurturance*

In order for possibility to be a constant in our lives we must become masters at creating an environment of safety and nurturance for ourselves. Granted, this sounds therapeutic and a bit unrealistic, nonetheless it is true and of the utmost importance if we are to achieve the life we want.

We come into this world having spent nine months in our mother's womb, which provided the essential elements of life, safety and nurturance. The ability to grow outside of the womb is the direct impact of our parent recreating an environment of safety and nurturance that then allowed for possibility.

As we leave our parents and enter the world, the responsibility for our safety and nurturance becomes our own.

- ◆ How safe is it in your head?
- ◆ How nurturing is your inner voice?
- ◆ How much possibility is in your life?

The Purpose of Talent

Your talents are meant to be shared

It has been said that our talents are a gift from life and what we do with them is our gift back to life.

Each of us possesses unique abilities that require attention. Just as a child must be nurtured, so must our talents. Just as a garden must be fertilized and freed of the burden of weeds to become a thing of beauty, so must our talents be developed.

Some choose to bury their talents, hide from the world out of fear of ridicule or failure while others choose to nurture, embrace and share their talents with others. Many people do nothing to nurture their talents because they desire the guarantees of an end result such as an occupation, career or reward. The truth is our talents provide no guarantees other than we will live with more passion and aliveness when we express them.

Some talents are destined to become our occupation while at other times this is not the case. Rather they are simply an expression of the gift of living life to the fullest.

When talents are left unexpressed this leads to a life of desperation and frustration. When expressed they lead to a life of achievement.

It is in the sharing and expression of our talent that passion is released and purpose is defined. To live a life of achievement, nurture your talents with dedication, belief, time and commitment.

The Truth About Luck

Luck is when opportunity and preparedness meet

They are so lucky! How often has this been said about successful people and high achievers? Is it that they are lucky or is it that they are prepared? It has also been said, "Luck is when opportunity and preparedness meet."

Preparation for our success has more to do with laying a foundation. It also takes developing skills, taking action, and enhancing our ability to be ready when a door opens rather than relying on simply a matter of luck.

Frequently we are offered opportunities we can choose to act upon or not. A door will open and we can either stand at the threshold or choose to walk through.

What holds some back is the fear of what is

unknown on the other side. The truth is every moment of our life is an unknown.

From the moment we rise in the morning to the moment we retire at night we cannot determine all we will experience in the day.

We can choose to stand at the threshold of life, hesitating to fulfill our deepest purpose, ever wondering what we could have achieved. Or we can choose to explore our talents and watch the wonder of our life unfold in such a way that others may be tempted to say, "They are so lucky!"

The Purpose of Experience

Experience is the best teacher

Experience is a great teacher, and yet an incident from the past can easily hold us back from exploring our future possibilities. Life carries with it an invisible line with past experiences on one side and future experiences on the other. The events of the past can either hold us back from our greatest potential or offer evidence of what is possible.

There is also possibility in an experience that we have yet to explore. For the fearful at heart the unknown details of a future situation can immobilize and prevent them from completely diving into the possibility of a full life. For the adventurous at heart the question that may arise is, "What kind of experience do I want?" or "How do I want to be remembered when all is said and done?"

Truly it is our experiences that make our life full or not. Every experience from our past was once a mystery of our future. A mystery that became a memory.

What are the experiences you choose to create that give you evidence of what you are capable of achieving? What will be the memories you leave behind for others through your experiences? What will you base your future choices on when creating experiences that become the portrait of your life?

The Purpose of Giving

It is in the giving we receive the greatest gift

Freely I was given, freely I give. A thought as old as time. During a Sunday sermon these words swell in the hearts of many, yet upon entering back into the world outside of the walls of a religious institute, many fail to heed this ancient message.

Truth is, whatever we give we tend to receive back tenfold. But how often do we hold back from giving when the opportunity arises? Whether it is time, money or love, we may hold back out of fear there will not be enough to go around. Or we may hold back as a way of keeping a check and balance with others. Perhaps our unwillingness to give is done out of a need for control.

And yet it is in the giving we often discover there is much to receive.

The opportunity to give is ever present. The paradox is, we cannot give what we do not have in the first place.

Even more perplexing to some is, what they most desire in life is what they most need to give away.

A simple thought to consider is this: to live a complete life and a life of ultimate purpose, we must be willing to give our best to every encounter we have.

Give all the love, honesty and joy you are capable of giving in each moment. Leave no stone unturned, no thought unsaid, no words unspoken to those you love so that each relationship is complete at all times. Freely share your knowledge with those who would benefit from it. Trust that when you give there is more for you to receive.

The Purpose of Failure

The greatest failure may be the limitations within our mind

A life of achievement isn't without failure. It is through failure that we are allowed opportunities to choose new paths and find the space to grow.

Success in virtually anything often requires failure in the very thing we desire to succeed at. In order to succeed we must be willing to fail. It is in the failure that we learn precisely what doesn't work. Learning from our failures brings us closer to achieving our desired results.

Infants and small children do not fear failure until they are taught to fear it. When they have a desire to walk, they do all they can to achieve the outcome regardless of how many times they fall. Falling could be considered failure to some, yet to a small child it simply means to get up and try again. As we grow and age, we develop a fear around falling, both figuratively and metaphorically.

It is in the ability to see why something hasn't worked and adjust accordingly that success is bound to occur. There may be a number of reasons why something doesn't work the way we think it should. At the time, we may not be ready to receive the goodness it will bring us. Consciously we may think we are, but on some level we are not. Perhaps there is more internal work to be done. Perhaps we are being led to trust the process of life more. Perhaps there are other areas that require our attention at the present time.

Consider this: life's delays are not life's denials. Life is about the experiences we have. In reality, we have often succeeded far more than we give ourselves credit. Perhaps we just refuse to see what we have done.

Take time to reflect on all the successes you have had. The success of walking, talking, loving, communicating, learning a skill you readily take for granted. All these abilities are ones that required some amount of failing, or falling, before you mastered them. Failure that turned into success.

"If something doesn't work, it's not a failure. It means you need to adjust and try, try, try again. Focus on how to make changes in order to achieve success."

Bev Kennedy 2005 - 2006 President
EWI Minneapolis Chapter

The Purpose of Intuition

*Intuition, a gut feeling, a hunch,
or just a sense*

Regardless of what we call it, each of us possesses the ability to intuitively know when something is right for us or not. This sense is designed to move us closer to our potential, possibility and purpose.

Intuition is the center of wisdom. It is the ability to trust a feeling or thought with no outward evidence. It is a knowing of what the correct action is to take.

When given the space to grow, this sense can guide us to areas of our being that we may consciously choose to ignore. Sadly, this sense is often disregarded due to our instinctive nature to be logical.

We may be given a thought or idea that for all outward appearances makes no sense, yet when explored takes us to a new level of our being.

We will be well served to take time to cultivate our inner sense. Begin with small steps. Explore the thoughts and ideas that bubble to a conscious level. Expand your possibilities of the unseen.

When we are open to possibility we are guided in amazing ways to our highest level of achievement.

The Purpose of the Spoken Word

Words have the power to move mountains

Sticks and stones may break my bones, but words will never hurt me. Never has a more false statement been made. Our words have incredible power to heal, nurture, encourage and manifest feelings of love. Conversely, our words have the power to wound, hurt and leave scars that are invisible to the naked eye.

The words we speak to others and within our mind are extremely powerful. They are the seeds that manifest possibility or fear.

We may not realize what we are saying or the power our words have on another. To achieve your greatest possibility make a commitment to only kind, nurturing, caring, encouraging and gentle words to others and to yourself.

Become conscious of the words you speak with a simple process of awareness and willingness. Awareness of every word that passes over your lips and a willingness to hold back harsh words that can leave a scar for life.

For today, choose words of kindness, love and hope.

The Purpose of Rest

Have we become so busy that rest is nonexistent?

Why is it that many of us have become too busy to simply rest? Could it be because rest seems to yield little to no visible signs of productivity? Rest, it seems, is something for the unoccupied; the lazy or the underachiever. Is this true or have we simply become so busy this is what we tell ourselves in order to justify the inability to relax?

We know we need our rest, but like sleep, we put it on the back burner and fill each hour with more important things. We have scheduled rest out of our day and we pay the price with emotional and creative deprivation.

When we do rest it is scheduled as some kind of main event. We take two weeks of vacation, filling every day with activities only to arrive back at home needing more rest. Businesses schedule "retreats" to escape the daily grind, but work hard at the retreat on what will be happening when they get back to work.

In the truest sense of the word, rest is freedom from activity. No phones, no chores, no meetings, nothing. Just rest. Many cultures schedule rest into their daily activities and considered it sacred.

It is in this place of freedom from activity we find the potential to achieve.

Let us take time to rest.

The Purpose of Balance

Ah, the joy of balance

There are brief moments in a life when all seems well; things seem in balance or perhaps, more accurately, we feel in balance.

Hopefully we are awake enough to cherish the experience and understand balance by its very nature exists as a result of a continual state of instability. Balance does not occur by placing even weights on a scale or by devoting even amounts of time to life's needs. Balance occurs by the recognition that with the demands of everyday life things will never be in perfect harmony and we make adjustments. It is in the acknowledgement that life will never be "perfect" that harmony is created.

When riding a bike we maintain our balance through

continual movement and readjustments. We maintain our life balance through the same process.

Balance is a dynamic process not a permanent state. We can move closer to a state of balance by consciously taking action whenever possible to create an environment of safety. An environment that speaks to our soul.

Through this process we find the balance that allows us to continue when the world becomes overwhelming.

The Purpose of Play

Play is so underrated

Watch a small child play and you quickly see it is through play that they learn new skills, how to interact socially, and most importantly they begin to understand who they are in relationship to the world and others. It is the benefit of self awareness and pure joy that exalts play to a necessary and life sustaining activity.

Play also results in achievement. Adults refer to it as "finding one's passion." Children simply say, "Let's go out and play." When your life's work has become synonymous with your play, miracles happen, results feel effortless and joy is a continual companion.

As adults sometimes we become so busy we no longer have time for the pleasures we enjoyed as children. Is it that we no longer have the time or we simply choose not to make the time?

A hidden treasure of play is that we rediscover what sparked our imagination years ago. Whether a long awaited bike ride, a roll in the grass, a game of hide and seek with a child, taking time to play not only sparks the imagination, it creates a sense of renewed energy.

It is in this renewed energy we can spark the flame of possibility.

A Place of Possibility

*Possibility lies in the potential to
fullfill our purpose*

Physical clutter lends itself to emotional and mental clutter. Or could it be the other way around?

From the discipline of simplicity to the art of feng shui, many practices tout the benefits of an orderly and simple space. Experts in creativity and productivity suggest cleaning your working and living spaces to allow for an influx of new ideas. We recommend doing the same to achieve your dreams.

Throw away anything you have not used in the last year; better yet, give it away. Declare a day and time that you will clear out the old and allow for the new.

When we create a vacuum, the universe will fill it. clean and order your space with a specific purpose in mind so that it will be filled with potential and possibility.

Possibility Based on Daily Decisions

*Every decision is a potential
seed to greatness*

We are faced with making decisions every day. Regardless of the situation, most people intuitively know what the correct decision is. Yet how often do we either fail to take action or make one that is not serving our highest purpose?

We can make the most appropriate decisions by clarifying what is important, what our values are, and what we want our contribution to be. With this insight we are in a position to make choices based on staying true to ourselves. It is in this truth our achievements are plentiful.

Not all correct choices are easy or without pain. There are occasions where making the right choice will require courage.

It has been said courage is not the absence of fear; it is the ability to identify the fear and walk through it anyway.

A life of possibility is one in which daily choices are made regardless of trepidations. It is in a life where decisions are made and acted upon that we find completeness.

"Achievement is a broad category that can be attained on a daily basis or even hourly basis. For the young child that learns how to climb a tree, to the senior citizen able to get out of bed in the morning, an achievement has been reached. Achievement is certainly in the heart of the achiever."

Joni Stoughton   2005 - 2006 President
EWI Austin Chapter

The Purpose of Acknowledgment

*Words can heal or wound long
after they are spoken*

Acknowledgement is like a mirror. When we acknowledge another they are given the gift of seeing a part of themselves that may have been hidden. It is through the eyes of another that we come face to face with our many dimensions. What a wonderful gift. The gift of acknowledging them in order that they know how much we appreciate them.

How often do people wait until something tragic happens before they tell another how much they appreciate them or what a wonderful contribution they make? Far too often, we get so caught up in day to day activities that we forget what can be most important: acknowledging the blessing that another person is in our life.

Acknowledgement is not to be reserved solely for our personal relationships. It is a cornerstone of a strong relationship among a work team.

When people feel their contributions are recognized and appreciated, the burden of the workload is lessened. The simple act of appreciating what a coworker, boss or peer contributes can work miracles.

Another aspect of acknowledgement is to recognize when we are going through a difficult time and allow others to be there for us. Whether we are struggling personally or professionally, what a gift we give to those who care about us when we ask for their help.

Acknowledgement is a well of endless possibility and potential. Acknowledge freely and frequently.

The Purpose of Contribution

*Life becomes complete when
your contribution is kindness*

The majority of the population has been born into an anxiety ridden culture that demands much of our time and energy. The quest for success leaves little time to generously contribute outside of our own personal sphere of influence. With multiple demands on our time we may choose self-interest over service. Ironically, the solution to too much self-interest is service to others.

The great paradox is, when we are feeling lonely, empty, unfulfilled and directionless, the quickest remedy is to get out of ourselves and into service.

A keen awareness of self occurs when authentic service is experienced. In a world that has become very "me" based, we lose sight of the incredible opportunities that contribution to something outside of ourselves can offer.

Too much energy, time or effort focused on self breeds self-centeredness. All you have to do is read a morning paper or listen to the evening news to acknowledge what self-centeredness can do to the demise of a community or nation.

Contribution can be done in small, unnoticed ways or on a larger scale. The truest gift of contribution is when it is made from the heart rather than from a place of showing others how wonderful we are. It is far more noble to be useful than it is to be wonderful.

The highest order of contribution is about self-less-ness. It grants us a life of greater meaning. Sad is the day we are too busy to contribute our time, energy and love. Let our commitment to a cause beyond ourselves be a guidepost to achievement.

"Each day a business professional is focused upon the multi-tasking needed to progress from one project to the next. No longer are we required to report if something is completed. Now we report - the numerous projects in process, expected completion dates, and what projects will be coming online.

Wouldn't it be grand if in our day-to-day activities we allotted for notation of achievements as they were occurring?

An achievement is after all a result gained by accomplishment no matter how large the impact."

Angela Telford 2005 - 2006 President
EWI Wichita Chapter

The Purpose of Creativity

Creativity is a journey of never ending discovery

Within each of us is a plethora of ideas waiting to be explored. There are levels of creativity yet untapped. How exciting life becomes when we allow our creativity to be expressed!

The highest of achievement is accomplished when we are willing to explore our ideas without attachment to the outcome. The very essence of creativity is the willingness to express ourselves with no expectation in return. In this journey we discover our greatest gifts.

When we allow ourselves to get lost in the experience of discovery we are often amazed at what unfolds. Problems are transformed into solutions and the impossible is made possible.

It has been said, "When there appears to be no

solution, that is when the solution will appear."
Creativity is simply about finding a solution where none
seems to exist.

There is a place within each of us where solutions
abound. A place where the answers dwell and we find
cooperation with self.

Through our problems we discover levels of
creativity we may not have tapped into previously.
Obstacles may reveal a level of achievement we never
knew existed.

*"Achievement is a result of having a professional and
personal network ready to solve problems with you and
offer advice."*

Linda White 2005 - 2006 President
EWI San Fernando Chapter

The Power of Respect

Possibility is revealed when one focuses on the simple concept of support and respect of others

Possibility is achieved in our ability to get along with others. We live in a diverse world made up of many different cultures, languages, races, and backgrounds. This kind of variety brings both challenges and blessings.

The challenges lie in the space of the unknown and unfamiliar. The blessings come from the same space.

As we look for possibility in this complex world, we should focus on the simple concept of support and respect for one another. Imagine if we could create an environment where differences are respected, opinions are valued, and all people are welcome.

Great achievements have been accomplished when respect is in the forefront of any relationship. As simplistic as it seems, treating people with respect simply makes the world a nicer place.

Because we live in a society that is highly competitive it is often easy to be disrespectful in order to place ourselves above others.

To respect another reminds our conscious awareness that we have more similarities than differences between us. The differences of nations, races and beliefs create a mosaic of possibility we can't experience in a homogenous world.

Make a conscious effort to create your day void of judgment and filled with respect.

The Purpose of Shifting Our Perception

Belief and possibility are based on perception

Most people know the difference between imagination and reality. Or do they? In fact, we can imagine something to be true, hold evidence of it in our mind and likely it becomes a reality.

You may have heard the phrase, "Perception is truth." Our beliefs are based on our perception. Whatever we believe to be true will become our truth.

Our beliefs either move us forward or hold us back. When steeped in a specific belief we may find it difficult to move beyond our current reality.

There will be occasions we are forced to evaluate our core beliefs, forcing us to shift our perceptions. There are also occasions we choose to willingly evaluate our beliefs and perception of reality without outward circumstances moving us to do so.

A life filled with possibility is one in which we consciously choose to evaluate what we believe to be true.

Today intentionally choose to evaluate your beliefs and perceptions and ask yourself, "Do they continue to serve my highest good? Are they allowing me to live on purpose?"

"One thing that makes a difference in my life is attitude. I approach everything as if it is possible. I look for stepping stones not stumbling blocks. The world is run by those who show up! Be a player!"

Brenda E. Humphrey 2005 - 2006 President
EWI Knoxville Chapter

The Purpose of Values

Honor your values and you honor your life

Values offer meaning to our life. They represent how people understand the world around them and they help to explain the world they experience.

In essence our values are our principles, standards, morals, ethics and the driving forces we live by. They shape our personal beliefs of right and wrong. It is in the representation of these beliefs that we find happiness or discontent.

Deep-set values are developed early in life and can be very resistant to change. They are developed out of direct experiences; especially with persons who influence us early in life such as parents, teachers, and religious or spiritual leaders. They are a driving force in everything you do.

Values can and will change as you go through the experience of living.

They may also change as you come to understand the reasons behind the values that others hold close to their heart. Those who are able to see beyond their own view of the world to a place of appreciation and acceptance of what is true to others are truly gifted.

In honoring your values you are honoring your personal path. In respecting other's values you honor their path and purpose.

The Purpose of Affirmations

Potential is determined by what is affirmed through thoughts and words

Affirmations are simple strategies for refocusing your thoughts and energy from a place of unclear direction to a place of clarity. Much has been said, written and taught about the power of affirmations to improve any given situation. Unfortunately, much of the information can be misleading and misguided.

Affirmations are simply words that affirm a specific outcome. They are the act of stating an outcome we declare to be true. They are simple tools that allow us to more readily access a state of possibility.

We are encouraged to make affirmative statements about ourselves that will build us up personally, professionally, emotionally, physically and spiritually. They are designed to give us a sense of value, strength and confidence.

There are self-affirmations and affirmations that come from others. Parents affirm for a child their belief of what the child is capable of. Often a child hears more about what they cannot do rather than what they can. Regardless of what is being said, insignificant statements by significant people are powerful.

Although the intention behind positive affirmations is noble, there is much evidence that in and of themselves, affirmations do little good. In order for an affirmation to be effective it must be believable and true to our conscious and, more importantly, subconscious mind.

Affirmations such as, "I can achieve whatever I want simply by affirming it," can actually cause more harm than good. There must be intention, action and some level of belief to support the statement. It is this combination that creates strong possibility.

A primary reason affirmations do not become reality is resistance. On some level we are resisting what we say we want. If our mindset is not one that supports the statement, then no matter what we do, we will not accomplish the outcome.

Affirmations are most effective when stated positively and in a way that they help to reveal our truth and our purpose.

Start your day with the following:

- Every day my purpose becomes clearer.
- My actions support a life of possibility.
- I choose to do that which supports my greatest potential.
- I am a loving and caring human being.

Take time each day to consciously affirm the direction you choose for your life. As you affirm your desired outcome, be willing to take the necessary action to make it a reality.

Possibility is Created by Thinking Big

The impossible is simply that which has not been attempted

How often do we hold ourselves back from our greatest potential because of uncertainty?

To achieve our greatest potential we must be willing to think big; to think beyond where we have dared to go before. We must become possibility thinkers. When possibility thinkers are faced with an obstacle they do not quit. They figure out how to go around, get over or go through the obstacle.

No matter what you read or hear about possibility thinking, the message comes back to the same point. Possibility thinkers see potential where none currently exists. They refuse to live a life of mediocrity. They have a clear understanding that we only go around once in this lifetime and we must make the most of it.

Possibility thinkers know that when you believe something is possible you will find the way to make it happen. They learn to see not just what is, but what can be.

Possibility thinkers do not let the evidence of outside forces deter them from moving toward their vision. If anything, obstacles are more of a motivator.

Consider this: two siblings are raised in the exact same limited environment. One sibling says the reason he did not accomplish all he could was due to his upbringing. The other sibling says the very thing that motivated him to accomplish all he did and be a person of contribution was due to his upbringing. What is the difference between the two? It is in the interpretation of their circumstances.

There are many circumstances in life we absolutely cannot change. However, by changing our attitude about the situation, we will be able to find possibility in even the most dire of circumstances.

The Purpose of Living in the Moment

"Someday" is the curse of those who believe they have forever to fulfill their purpose

"We must not allow the clock and the calendar to blind us to the fact that each moment of life is a miracle and mystery."

H. G. Wells (1866 - 1946)

How often do we chant the mantra, "someday"? Someday I will apply for that position. Someday I will go back to school. Someday I will begin eating healthy. Someday I will call my long lost friends.

It is the belief of fools that someday will arrive. The point of power is in the now; in the ability to live in the moment. If we wait for all circumstances to be "just right," chances are we will take minimal, if any, action.

Moments are lost amid the clutter of every day life.

They become blurred by the activities we invent. It seems like activity has become more important than the moments in which they occur. We focus on the quantity of activity we can squeeze into one 24-hour period rather than striving for moment-by-moment quality.

We are frequently caught up in the busyness of the day only to realize the day slipped by us. We dwell on what happened in the past or what might occur in the future, missing the magic of the ever present moment.

By simply shifting our focus from how much we can do to how much quality we can bring, we create the ability to craft magical memories. Although we have all heard, and even said, "Today is the only day we have," this belief is quickly forgotten. When a young child asks for a moment of our time, how often do we say we are too busy? When our spouse ask for some help with a simple matter, how often do we get frustrated because we couldn't watch every moment of our favorite television program?

There is power in periodically stopping what you are doing, giving thanks for the moment, and realizing it is this moment that makes up the fabric of your life. The awareness of the power of the moment allows us to become fully in tune with our purpose and power.

It is in the awareness and acceptance that *someday is today.*

"Achievement is when you focus on all the things that can go right rather than focusing on what can go wrong. Such a perspective keeps the spotlight on what's important and ultimately helps in all aspects of life."

Susan Burke President 2005 - 2006

EWI Salt Lake City Chapter

Potential in Uncertainty

Power can be found in uncertainty

M any people believe all would be well if they could just predict everything that will happen in their life. The truth is power can be found in uncertainty. Uncertainty allows us the ability to stretch our imagination and explore uncharted territory.

Today, more than ever, there is a greater need for flexibility in our thinking and actions. From one moment to the next things can radically change, requiring mental and physical shifts in a moment's notice.

Every day is a day of uncertainty. In virtually every environment we are required to do more with less. We are required to consistently learn information that will be obsolete with lightning speed. New technologies, economic uncertainty, global changes and new methods of communication have created both unprecedented challenges and opportunities.

The ability to capitalize on uncertainty is truly a gift of those with the greatest potential. They realize that each passing day holds more uncertainty in the world and are able to maintain a vision for the future. It is also about being prepared, to the best of their ability, for the unknowns that may occur. This involves gaining insights, information and road maps to assist in any change that may occur.

One of the greatest tools in dealing with the unknown is trust. Trust that even in the times of the greatest uncertainty we will get to the other side of any situation with more clarity of our purpose.

It is in the uncertainty that we are gifted with the opportunity to discover more about who we are than we ever dreamed possible.

Marketability and Possibility

Marketability creates unlimited possibility

In today's ever changing world one of the most essential skills is that of marketability. Many people hold the belief that marketability is a corporate issue only. Businesses are concerned with marketing plans and strategies, always watching the bottom line for marketing success.

As much as organizations must be able to market their products, services and philosophies, so must an individual. This skill alone creates unlimited possibility.

Many object to the thought of marketing themselves feeling only the brazen and aggressive dare to be so bold. Regardless of whether you own a business, run a nonprofit association or work for a company, the landscape has changed. Security is an illusion.

Marketability simply put is the law of attraction. It is a quality of energy others want to participate in. Marketability is the ability to communicate possibility.

"Achievement is the successful accomplishment of making dreams a reality through the setting of spiritual, professional or personally defined short and long term goals, while overcoming any obstacles presented along the way."

La Donna A. Sims 2005 - 2006 President
EWI Fort Wayne Chapter

The Purpose of a Circle of Influence

Possibility is created by what you know and who you know

In virtually any environment there is what is known as a "circle of influence." We have all heard, "It's not what you know, but who you know that matters." In fact both determine your level of possibility.

More often than not, when you need the services of a specific professional you turn to friends, family and associates for recommendations and referrals. A strong possibility for success is determined by how large and wide your reach is. Most have a reach of several hundred people.

Each of the people in your circle knows several hundred people. Those people know several hundred people. When you think about the reach potential it can be mind boggling.

Virtually anything you need is within a very short reach through your circle of influence. You are also in a position to help those who are within your sphere of influence as the opportunity arises.

As with anything, it is essential to nurture the relationships in your network. Sadly, many people only connect with others when they need something. Great power lies in connecting on a regular basis.

Think about your own circle of influence. What have you done lately to nurture and develop these relationships? Put time and effort into them and watch the magic happen.

"Achievement is a result of having a network of professionals who help each other succeed in professional and personal endeavors. When you make connections and form friendships that last a lifetime you achieve something incredible."

Kris Sheraski 2005 - 2006 President

EWI St. Paul Chapter

Purpose Through Contemplation

Sit quiet allowing your purpose to evolve

One of the most profound and important questions we can ask ourselves is, "What is my purpose?" With so much taking up our time, we do not stop long enough to contemplate this incredibly vital question.

Virtually every belief system seeks to provide us with an answer. In some spiritual practices it is believed that all suffering is a result of striving to obtain things that do not bring us happiness. We are determined to hold on to things of the material nature. Because they do not last, we cannot find eternal happiness in these things nor can we find our purpose. Even in our relationships we often try to hold on in ways that are not possible.

Each of us has a purpose for being here and a special gift that is unique to us. We only need delve into that place in our spirit that allows us to go beyond the busyness of our day or the limitations of our bodies to discover our truth.

Consider this: our purpose may very well be a direct result of all the circumstances that have led us to this point in our life. It is the changes that are forced upon us by the circumstances of life that allow us to fully grow into our purpose. The resistance to our purpose can bring us sorrow, loneliness, and feelings of regret.

It is in the discovery of our path and the acceptance of what we have been tasked with that we find true happiness.

Achievement Through Physical Energy

The more energy we have the more we are able to achieve

The physical body is an amazing instrument of power, yet many do not utilize it to their greatest ability. It isn't about how much muscle mass one has or how "beautiful" one is. It is about accessing energy in the ultimate fashion.

An established truth is that the more energy we have the more we are able to achieve. Unfortunately, most of us do not do what we can to optimize our energy. Imagine how much more we would be able to achieve if we had double the energy. Rather than thinking about what we want to do we would simply do it.

Another characteristic of physical energy is how we carry our bodies. Notice how you feel when you are slouched compared to when there is height in the way you carry yourself. How we feel in our bodies makes a night and day difference between how you feel and view your possibilities.

Increasing our energy takes focus, commitment and dedication. As with anything, it is all about choice. The choice to eat healthy… or not. The choice to exercise… or not. The choice to do what is ultimately the best for us… or not.

Achieving Success

Gauge success not merely by one criteria

For many people, the definition of success is closely associated with money. Those who focus solely on financial successes will be out of balance and ultimately disappointed.

There is nothing wrong with having money; the more you have the more you can do for yourself, others, and society at large. However, if that is your only criteria for success, there is a good chance the rest of your life will suffer.

Success and achievement demand a personal equilibrium or else we quickly burn out. A balanced life offers more possibilities and greater potential than a life that is narrow in focus.

Success includes many things at different times in your life:

- A balance between family and career
- Contentment
- Emotional well-being
- Happiness
- Health
- Love
- Making a positive impact in the lives of others
- Self-development
- Self-respect
- Spiritually

Appreciating and Acknowledging Our Successes

Through self-appreciation we expand our possibility of all appreciation

It is important to acknowledge what we have achieved in life even if nobody else does. Self-acknowledgement lays the ground work for new and grander possibilities. It is hard to continually grow and expand without a cheering section and we should be our greatest fan.

Do not mistake self-appreciation with boastfulness or false pride. It is about self-love. By acknowledging our achievements we assert that we are capable and competent, able to handle what life has to offer. Each achievement builds on the next leaving us to trust our knowledge, skills, and ultimately ourselves.

No one starts out on the road of achievement, but through practice and support we learn to maneuver and measure our successes. We learn that failure is as important as success; it offers feedback and an opportunity to make the necessary corrections to our path.

All possibilities hold both success and failure as outcomes. When we acknowledge our willingness to explore and express possibilities, our failures don't hurt as much and the success feels great!

"Our success in life lies solely in our achievements."
Barbara K. Kenshalo President 2005 - 2006
EWI Denver Chapter

The Potential in Time

Choose wisely in the here and now

There is not enough time. There is just too much to do, calls to make, people to see.

We feel over-worked and underpaid. There are not enough resources to do the job. Multiple projects and priorities eat away at our day. Day timers, organizers and palm pilots assist us in the efficient use of our time. Traffic reports guide us to work; weather reports prepare us for the ride home. We punch into a time clock or we are exempt and never punch out.

Is it so difficult managing time or is our expectation for achievement so high that the 24 hours in a day is simply not enough?

It is so easy to waste time and never recapture a missed moment. Where you spend your time determines how you live your life; in peace or in turmoil, in love or in fear.

One of the few things we truly possess is time. There is only so much you can do and only so many roles you can play. How we choose to use the here and now is a personal and a powerful choice. Choose wisely.

Living an Involved Life

*Passion is created through the
full engagement of your life*

Get involved in your life. Sounds funny, doesn't it?
All joking aside, the greater your involvement in
your life, the greater the achievements.

Like many endeavors of personal growth, it is easy
to check-out, giving our power to others.

How do we check-out of our life, leaving it to the
direction of others?

We disconnect and disassociate in many ways.

- Too busy
- Over committed
- Submission
- Too tired
- Under enthused
- Apathetic

To be actively engaged in life we must make ourselves a priority. Not at the cost of others, but with the clear intention that our life holds the same potential and possibilities as anyone else.

If you knew your abilities and dreams of achievement would change the world for the better, would you act on them?

Achieving Our Dreams

*Goals are merely dreams with a
timeframe in mind*

A method to building high self-esteem and promoting achievement is to be committed to our dreams. When dreams come true we feel a sense of the divine in our lives.

When we hear someone declare, "I'm living my dream," a part of us may sigh in envy or in gratitude. We are envious if we've not achieved our dreams or we are grateful that another has achieved theirs. We know that when someone is living their dream, achievement is easy and days are filled with happiness.

We all revel in the thought of waking each morning with joy in our heart, energy in our step, and walking out the front door and into our life's dream. Living a life on purpose requires we have a dream and dreams require risks.

Authenticity

A state of truth

Is authenticity a natural state? Or is authenticity achieved as a result of living a long life filled with many experiences that define who we are?

Do children grow out of being authentic or do adults cloak their authenticity to protect the sense of vulnerability that comes with the territory? Have we become a society with an attitude of "I don't want to know who you are and I certainly don't want you to know me."? Is it strange that when someone calls us authentic we take it as a compliment?

Regardless of which is true, it is evident that authenticity has a quality of the mysterious; some of us striving for it and others masking it at all costs. It is difficult to build a life of achievement and continual possibilities based upon a false self.

No matter how grand our accomplishments, if we are not acting authentically, they become a house of cards ready to collapse at a moment's notice.

A false self is a natural enemy and will eventually sabotage all you do and turn all achievements into failure.

Live your truth.

Honoring Our Values

*Values are the measuring stick
by which we live*

Identifying our values is one of the most important things we can do for ourselves. Values are a guiding force in our life. Without them we are tossed about without direction and perpetually off course.

It is important to not only identify our values; we must honor them in order to live by them. Hold them close to your heart, share them with others and speak to them when they beckon your voice.

Standing up for what we value is one of the greatest achievements in life. Entire populations have stood to the side as their values were questioned and ultimately destroyed.

Like water on stone, our values can be eroded. One lapse in judgment followed by another leads to a weak constitution. Prolonged weakness leads to defeat.

True achievement comes from intuitively knowing what guides us and having the willingness to honor this.

It has been said, "When it's the right thing to do, it is the right thing to do."

Doing what is right is born from a place of love, honor and integrity.

Perfection and Achievement

Strive for progress rather than perfection

Possibilities cannot and will not surface when there is a demand for perfection. Perfection is a killer of dreams and the enemy of achievement. So many suffer under the expectation of perfection. We would almost prefer paralysis rather than embracing a possibility only to be disappointed by our inability to generate the perfect outcome.

Perfection is fear manifest. It will only feed one's anxiety and amplify our sense of inadequacy.

Give up perfection, embrace action and see where the world takes you!

Potential in the Now

We all have the same amount of time

Some people seem to utilize their time effectively and others seem to be so far behind they will never catch up. Time can be a gift or a culprit. It can provide us with a sense of achievement or frantic urgency.

The questions each of us must ask are, "Am I using my time in my best interest, to the best of my ability?" and "Is time an ally used for the purpose of appreciating life, a tool for possibility in my life, or is time my nemesis - something to struggle against and resist?"

For all of us who struggle with time it seems ironic when confronted with mortality. The first question we ask is, "How much time do I have?"

You have today. This hour. This moment. That's it. No assurances of tomorrow. No way to recapture yesterday. All you have is NOW.

The Wonder of Work

Blessed are those who love their work

We measure the health of the economy based upon how many people are working. From the State of the Union to the state of our local affairs, work determines the health of our nation, community, town, home, and self.

We educate our children so they can find meaningful work. We want them to have a life of achievement and work that is fulfilling. What this really means is we want them to have peace, to avoid anxiety, to enjoy their life. We want them to have options, possibilities and the freedom to express their potential.

That is why work and the state of employment are as important to us as a nation and a family. It is a road to freedom and expression. There are fewer joys than having a job that fulfills your purpose and being well compensated for it.

"Achievement is the result of compassion, pride, hard work, and believing in each other."

Peachie Bailey 2005 - 2006 President
EWI Memphis Chapter

Willing to Expand

Expand into your greatness

So much of life is a choice between expansion and contraction. As much as we'd like to think we are continually learning and expanding into new possibilities, it's amazing how easy it is to contract and settle for less.

Many people live a life with the small and cramped feeling of contracting, achieving far less than they are capable of.

The danger in settling is you never know what you've settled for until it is too late. To settle will rob years from your life. To settle conjures an environment of negativity that will leave you weary and lifeless.

Expanding requires movement. It could be as simple as taking one step in a new direction. Practice expansion on a daily basis. Avoid the mundane.

Intuition

Trust the process, trust yourself

For many, achievement centers around their intuition, an inner knowing as to what to do and when to do it. Listening to your intuition is something many people ignore. It's not just about women's intuition, it's about human intuition.

We usually know on some level what to do in any particular situation. We may get a feeling, hear a message or get a picture in our mind's eye. We know what the right action to take is, but for whatever reason, choose to ignore our intuition. When we do this, we invalidate our inner wisdom. It's as if we don't trust our own judgment.

Our intuition is a gift which is meant to guide us. When we ignore our instincts we may find ourselves faced with unnecessary difficulties or even going in the opposite direction than the one we had intended. When we trust our intuition we will find that life's travels are much softer.

Honor what you know to be true.

Abundance and Achievement

Make the decision and watch life support you

Abundance is the result of our emotions and beliefs being in harmony. As complicated and random as life seems, there are times when we are acutely aware of the synchronistic and coincidental nature of our thoughts and experience.

You think of someone and they call a moment later; you're looking for a lost item and coincidentally it appears out of nowhere; you make a decision and life provides the resources to support that decision. What if what we consider coincidental and synchronistic is really a result of our thinking matched by circumstances?

Take a leap of faith and for 30 days mind your emotions, beliefs and thoughts. Make a conscious effort to keep your thoughts and emotions positive breaking a habit of negative and anxious thinking. By the end of the 30 days you'll notice life is lighter, coincidence is commonplace and you're achieving a lot more than you believed possible.

A Prayer of Possibility

*Prayer is the feeling rather than
the words*

Every day offers the possibility of a life filled with achievement. Our thoughts and prayers set the context for our day and direct our attention.

We've found the following prayer to be particularly uplifting and appropriate to the setting the stage for a day filled with possibility and potential.

Good Morning !
Thank you for this wonderful day before me.

I receive this day as the GIFT that it is,
full of JOY, LOVE, LAUGHTER
and PEACE

I accept ABUNDANCE in ALL areas
of my life and I say thank you in advance
for a happy and prosperous day.

I accept with GRATITUDE
total and perfect health as every cell in my
body radiates perfect LOVE.

I JOYFULLY release this day
Knowing that you walk with me in
every moment, showing me where to go,
who to see and what to say.

My life radiates perfect joy, perfect love,
perfect health and perfect peace.

I greet this day on purpose,
ready to achieve and accept my best!

Michelle Butz

Grateful Achievement

The highest emotional vibration is that of gratitude

The practice of gratitude is by far one of the most powerful acts you can do to live a life of achievement and possibility.

Abundance is linked to achievement and both are the result of a positive and anticipatory emotional state. Gratitude is the highest emotional state you can live in, turning the mundane into the miraculous and the ordinary into the extraordinary.

Keep a gratitude journal for 30 days and watch what coincidental or synergistic events occur. Your journal will keep you focused and grateful. Focusing on gratitude keeps your emotional state high and the experience of your daily events blessed. Gratitude creates endless possibilities.

Start your mornings with a list of those things you are grateful for and end your day the same way. The events of your day will be surrounded in grace, turning an average consciousness and a typical life into a life of achievement and a consciousness of possibility.

The Purpose of Worth

Worth is measured more by character than outward possessions

We live in a society of "measured worth" where we assess our achievement by material standards of wealth. Unfortunately, a person can be monetarily wealthy and still live in an experience of emotional poverty; seeking acceptance only to find unrelenting expectations and continual disappointment. Regardless of how extravagant a lifestyle or luxurious one's material possessions are, in the absence of self-love, monetary wealth is shallow and true achievement elusive.

To live from a place of worth is to recognize our wholeness. It is to live from a place of sufficiency not from a place of being incomplete. Hypnotized to believe we've come to the game of life inherently flawed, it can be difficult to find the energy to achieve and the steadfastness to live on purpose.

How do we find this inner strength? Surround yourself with people who love you, people who can see who you are when you cannot.

Those individuals speak to your worth, inspiring you into action and achievement. They are your coaches holding success while you train for the game.

"Achievement is a result of leaving a positive, lasting impression with those we interact with, both personally and professionally. When we have somehow assisted others or simply brightened their day we have accomplished something great."

Kimberly McLain 2005 - 2006 President
EWI Harrisburg Chapter

A Journal of Evidence

*Notice what is working rather
than what is not*

A practice of achievement is often initiated by the desire of a specific experience. Whether it is starting a business, excelling at a sport, being a wonderful parent or spouse, or achieving complete relaxation, the minute we declare a desire the mind looks for evidence as to why we can't have it and the unlikelihood of it actually manifesting in our life. We are taught to assess progress by what is not working rather than what is working.

An *Evidence Journal* is designed to list all signs, large or small, of the inevitable manifestation of your desires. On a daily basis, list all events, occurrences, coincidences or any other indication of the arrival of your goal. Every time you list evidence, celebrate and be happy. Anticipate the next milestone. Any kind of achievement requires a prolonged state of faith. Your *Evidence Journal* will speed your journey.

"When one achieves a goal, it is usually because they have overcome or conquered some sort of fear or trepidation that was associated with the goal. High achievers either have no fear or they don't admit it."

Diane Eicher 2005 - 2006 President
EWI Los Angeles Chapter

A Prayer of Potential

Give thanks

No more powerful a prayer than, "Thank You!"

No more powerful a thought than, "Thank You!"

No more powerful a state than, "Thank You!"

No more powerful a life than one of thanks!

Achievement May Mean Less

Simplicity may be the greatest achievement of all

Over achievement can lead to too much of one thing resulting in not enough of something else. Too much competition can lead to not enough collaboration. Too grand a desire to win can lead to a sense of loss. Too much of anything creates its own kind of poverty.

In order to achieve our hearts desires, there will be times when we must simplify, boil life down to the necessities, eliminate distractions and find our bearings. Often an absence of one thing allows for the achievement of something else.

What can you rid yourself of in order to achieve more?

Every Day Is a New Possibility

Each day holds the potential for achievement

The rising of the sun brings new opportunities and new possibilities. Each night we let go of the day and turn our intention to the coming of a new time. Possibilities lurk in the shadows as we drift off to sleep; they stir our hearts and awaken our minds for what is to come.

The daily possibilities may not be grand, but like a hologram, each day is a part of an entire lifetime. Do not underestimate the impact of small dreams and daily actions. Each new dream of achievement opens our heart and each action builds upon the other to eventually deliver a lifetime worthy of praise.

"Achievement is a direct result of positive thinking. The stronger your power of positive intention, the more likely you are to achieve the results you want. If you keep your mind focused on achieving your goals, there's nothing you can't achieve."

Sue Miner 2005 - 2006 President

EWI Spokane Chapter

Completion and Achievement

Achievement demands completion

Life has a way of tugging at our attention, pulling us in different directions and leading us in circles. At times it seems hard to complete what we've started and finish what is in front of us. Sometimes we must fight for the right to complete things, asking others to be patient and disciplining ourselves to be focused.

We must assert our will and resist the tide of a busy life in order to have a satisfying life. There is a satisfaction in completion and that is the experience of achievement.

When tasks and dreams find their way to completion, we breath easier, have something visible to account for our effort, and have a trust in ourselves that we can complete what we start.

The Purpose of Optimism

Sooth your soul with an optimistic mind

High achievers are usually optimistic. More than an exercise of the mind, high achievers have either taught themselves to be positive or were raised in an optimistic environment. Expecting the best became second nature to them.

Optimism is soothing to the soul. It brings a certain peace as we embrace our purpose and strive to achieve our goals. Even mistakes are viewed by the optimistic as a blessing in disguise and a step closer to their ultimate achievement. We admire the optimistic and seek their company. We know the power of a positive mind and an optimistic heart.

Choose to be optimistic and live a life of achievement.

The Energy of Achievement

*Great joy is a result of achieving
our dreams*

There are many qualities of energy that drive achievement. Some achieve out of anger, determined to prove others wrong. Some achieve out of envy wanting what others have. Then there are those who achieve out of pure joy. The joy of being able to craft a life of accomplishments and live a life of purpose.

The energy of joy is so attractive others gravitate to it, satisfied to bask in the presence of joy and the person who exudes it.

To achieve with joy is easy though not without effort. Similar to serving, the gift of joy is always greater for the one who is giving and the achievement is a secondary bonus.

Humility

*It is in the ability to serve one
may discover their purpose*

People who have changed the world for the better are achievers of the highest degree. It doesn't matter if they are personal or global heroes, the ability to change the hearts and minds of men takes a humility and understanding few possess.

Humility is reserved for the truly great; they know that of themselves they are nothing. They all possess a belief in something greater than self and a burning desire to serve.

Many heroes of generations or cultures past have humbled us by their achievements. They seek no praise because they understand their achievements are intrinsically related to the needs at hand. Their ability to fill those needs is their gift.

It is in a place of humility one can experience their greatest potential.

"Regardless whether you are rich or poor, as you travel thru your journey of life, challenges and opportunities are presented to you. Unselfishly handling these to the best of your ability, and having a positive impact on the lives of others defines achievement."

Nancy Wallace   2005 - 2006 President
EWI Dallas Chapter

Generosity

Give in order to receive

A high form of achievement is to live a generous life. Achievement brings rewards and those rewards are to be shared.

When we give to others we are rewarded in many ways and by many people.

The gift of generosity need not be monetary; it may simply be a good deed, a kind word, or an hour of companionship. Your generosity may not be returned from the same person, but be assured that the universe loves a generous person and will send it back tenfold.

A life that is marked by generosity is a life that is filled with purpose, possibility and potential.

Achievement for Achievement's Sake

Achievement allows for contribution

Achievement for achievement's sake is ultimately a journey with a dead end.

We know the self is demanding and will continuously hunger for more. The adrenaline of achievement becomes addictive when done only with our best interest in mind, but like any addiction, there is a price. We disconnect from a purpose grander than ourselves and waste our gifts on an ego that is never satisfied.

To be self-centered is void of purpose and empty of possibility.

When our achievements contribute to the well-being of a community, a family or another, our purpose is realized and everything is possible.

Greatest Achievement

Achievement lives in the heart of our family

Achievements aren't always tasks, competitions or acquisitions. Ask many parents and they will say their greatest achievement is their child or children. What a grand opportunity to usher another human being into the world. What an achievement to care for and about another only to let them go and experience the world on their own.

The job of providing shelter to another, offering love and possibilities, is by far one of the grander things in the scheme of life. We don't need to search for Olympic Gold to be a high achiever. We may find our greatest achievement under the roof of our home and in the hearts of our family.

"When accomplishments are not remembered today, but will be long remembered after tomorrow by someone other than yourself, you have found your purpose."

Debra Gale Byars 2005 - 2006 President

The Last Achievement

Live today as if it is your only day

It all will end one day. Life as we know it is destined to change. Our bodies will no longer house our heart's desires and signs of our achievements will hang on a wall as a distant memory.

We will leave this earth. How and when we leave is a mystery. Until then, our life is in our hands. We are free to explore possibilities, express our potential and live our purpose.

Life's achievements will pass and all that remains is the memory of the love we've left in the hearts of others.

Our desire in writing this book is that we will remain a gentle reminder in your heart. Our desire for you is that you will leave a gentle reminder in the hearts of many.

"Your life will either be a warning of what not to do or a stellar example of what is possible. You choose moment by moment. Choose wisely."
~ Kathleen Gage ~

Executive Women International

We invite you to be a part of Executive Women International (EWI) -- the leading connection for business professionals. EWI was established in 1938 to provide businesswomen from diverse industries a forum for promoting their firms, enhancing their personal and professional development and engaging in community activities. Today, EWI has 75 chapters and 3,000 members across the United States, Canada, and Europe who remain committed to bringing value to its firms, to benefiting the careers of its representatives and to providing service to EWI communities.

Why join EWI? There are a myriad of reasons and one is the perfect fit for you:

- Gain new leadership skills through landmark on-site and on-line training programs and opportunities for volunteer leadership.
- Build awareness of your company locally, nationally, and internationally and be recognized as a business leader.
- Build your business through the valuable EWI network which includes an on and offline International Directory.
- Get involved in your community through EWI philanthropic initiatives such as the Reading Rally.

Members will tell you that EWI is much more than a business networking organization. Long term and valuable business relationships and friendships are established as members discover unique opportunities to work together both in the office, and in the community. For more information about EWI, its programs, and membership go to **executivewomen.org**.

The authors extend a special thanks to the Board of Directors of Executive Women International and the Corporate Staff for your support and belief in The Law of Achievement.

The Reading Rally

Since 1992, EWI has been committed to promoting literacy through annual Reading Rallies hosted by EWI Chapters throughout the organization.

EWI's signature event, conducted with community groups, schools, and national associations, promotes reading to children. Chapters host a variety of programs that range from community read-ins and book donations to major events involving celebrities, story characters, and the creation of reading rooms. More than 700 EWI volunteers work with approximately 20,000 children at schools, crisis centers, hospitals, and community organizations during Reading Rally events each year.

To learn more about the Reading Rally and find out what is happening in your local area visit executivewomen.org.

A portion of each book sale will be donated to Executive Women International's Reading Rally.

 Described by many as one of the most inspirational speakers alive, Kathleen Gage, known as the "Street Smarts" speaker, teaches others how to use instinct, wit, creativity, and spirit to achieve their fullest potential.

Although Kathleen is recognized as a top leader in her field, this wasn't always the case. Kathleen made choices in her teens and early twenties that took her from a comfortable middle-class upbringing to a life of homelessness and being unemployable.

Kathleen Gage rose above seemingly insurmountable odds to become an award winning business owner, author, sales and marketing trainer, and keynote speaker.

Living for extended periods of time on the West Bank of Israel and Mexico, overcoming a bout with paralysis at a young age and living through the great quake of 1985 in Mexico City, Kathleen has a unique understanding of the delicate balance of life.

The recipient of numerous awards for outstanding achievement, Kathleen was recognized in 2004 by the governor of her state as one of their top business owners. She has also been honored with the

Communication and Leadership Award by Toastmasters International and was twice recognized as Member of the Year by the National Speakers Association, Utah Chapter.

Kathleen has dedicated her life to assisting others in unleashing possibilities to create a life rich in spirit, passion, prosperity, self-assurance, and success; all the rewards of living a life of achievement.

Kathleen@TurningPointPresents.com
www.KathleenGage.com

To subscribe to Kathleen's complimentary online newsletter visit www.kathleengage.com

Other resources by Kathleen Gage

Books
* 101 Ways to Get Your Foot in the Door
* Message of Hope, Inspirational Thoughts for Uncertain Times
* Workplace Miracles, Inspiring Stories and Thoughts of Possibility

eProducts/Multi Media programs
* Street Smarts Marketing & Promotions; Success Strategies for Marketing a Small Business on a Limited Budget
* Street Smarts Making Money on the Internet
* Keys to Creating Profitable Events
* 101 No Cost & Low Cost Ways to Market a Product, Service or Business

Audio tapes and CDs
* Living Life With Serenity
* Confidence and Credibility Through High Self Esteem
* The Power Within Us
* The Softer Side of Success

Kathleen@TurningPointPresents.com
www.KathleenGage.com

 As a nationally recognized speaker and author, Lori Giovannoni has shared the platform with other authors, entrepreneurs and leaders throughout the world. During her career, Lori has had the opportunity to address over 250,000 people in 47 states, Canada and Puerto Rico.

Before becoming a full-time author and speaker, Lori was Legislative Director for the California Chamber of Commerce and Executive Director of the California Association of Chamber of Commerce Executives.

A highly accomplished business owner, Lori was recognized as the Athena Recipient - Business Woman of the Year (2001 - 2002) in the state of Utah, and one of 30 Women to Watch in 2005 by Salt Lake Business Magazine.

In the year 2000, Lori was diagnosed with breast cancer and now joins the ranks of cancer survivors. She has been a tireless advocate for raising awareness and funds for breast cancer research.

Lori is the Chief Operating Officer for the Western Institute of Spirituality and Healing in Medicine (SHIM). SHIM is an organization dedicated to raising awareness of the power of spirituality in medicine.

Lori has the unique ability to deliver insight and wisdom in a way few others possess. She is viewed as a visionary within the speaking field and has a keen ability to assist others to be the best they can be.

Lori is a highly sought after speaker for corporate training and conferences throughout the nation.

Her message is clear - Kindness is the greatest gift we can give others.

Lori@xmission.com
www.LoriGiovannoni.com

Other resources by Lori Giovannoni

Books
- Success Redefined, Notes to a Working Women
- 101 Ways to Get Your Foot in the Door
- Workplace Miracles, Inspiring Stories and Thoughts of Possibility

Multi Media programs
- Presentations for Profit
- Professional Presentation Skills
- Earn More Than Ever Before

Audio Tapes and CDs
- Leadership Skills
- Staying Marketable in an Ever Changing Economy
- High Achievement Behavior
- The Softer Side of Success

Lori@xmission.com
www.LoriGiovannoni.com